SPIDERS SET II

HOBO SPIDERS

Jill C. Wheeler
ABDO Publishing Company

visit us at
www.abdopub.com

Published by ABDO Publishing Company, 4940 Viking Drive, Edina, Minnesota 55435.
Copyright © 2006 by Abdo Consulting Group, Inc. International copyrights reserved in all
countries. No part of this book may be reproduced in any form without written permission from
the publisher. The Checkerboard Library™ is a trademark and logo of ABDO Publishing
Company.

Printed in the United States.

Cover Photo: Joe Belknap, Big H Products, Inc, www.HoboSpider.com
Interior Photos: Animals Animals pp. 5, 15, 16; Jim Kalisch, University of Nebraska pp. 9, 17;
    Joe Belknap, Big H Products, Inc, www.HoboSpider.com pp. 7, 11, 13, 19, 21

Series Coordinator: Stephanie Hedlund
Editors: Tamara L. Britton, Stephanie Hedlund
Art Direction: Neil Klinepier

Library of Congress Cataloging-in-Publication Data

Wheeler, Jill C., 1964-
    Hobo spiders / Jill C. Wheeler.
        p. cm. -- (Spiders. Set II)
    Includes bibliographical references.
    ISBN 1-59679-295-7
    1. Hobo spider--Juvenile literature. I. Title.

    QL458.42.A3W44 2006
    595.4'4--dc22

                                                                            2005045736

CONTENTS

HOBO SPIDERS

Hobo spiders are among the world's 34,000 species of spiders. All spiders are **arachnids**. Scorpions, ticks, and mites are arachnids, too. All arachnids are **arthropods**.

Hobo spiders used to be found only in Europe. There, they earned the name *Tegenaria agrestis* or "mat weaver of the field." Today, hobo spiders also live in North America. These spiders were first found around Seattle, Washington, in the 1930s.

Hobo spiders belong to the funnel weaver **family** Agelenidae. There are about 700 species of spiders in this family.

All funnel weaver spiders share several **traits**. They can move quickly. They also weave a funnel-like pocket at the back of their webs. Funnel weaver spiders sit quietly in these pockets waiting for their prey.

Researchers believe hobo spiders came to the United States on a ship from Europe. The ship probably had a hobo spider egg case on board, much like this funnel weaver spider's egg case.

Sizes

Hobo spiders are bigger than most spiders. They are usually 15/32 to 23/32 of an inch (12 to 18 mm) long. Female hobo spiders are larger than males.

The hobo spider's legs can stretch up to two inches (5 cm). But even with these long legs, an average hobo spider could still fit on a silver dollar coin.

Bites from hobo spiders can cause problems. Most people do not feel the bite at all. The bite creates a small hard place on the skin. It turns into a large, red, blistered area in about a day.

The bite can cause scarring and skin damage if not treated. Some doctors claim hobo spider bites can be deadly. But, the **venom** of the hobo spider may not be the problem.

Researchers have learned that hobo spiders may carry **bacteria** on their fangs. It is this bacteria that makes the bite so harmful.

If you live near the hobo spider, be careful what you reach into. You could end up shaking hands with a hobo spider!

SHAPES

Hobo spiders have eight long, hairy legs. They have two hairy body parts. The head and **thorax** make up the front body part. It is called the **cephalothorax**. The wide, rear body part is called the abdomen.

Like all spiders, a hobo spider has two **pedipalps** at the front of its cephalothorax. The pedipalps look like short legs. Male hobo spiders have a swelling at the end of each of their pedipalps. These swellings look like boxing gloves.

There are also two other leglike organs at the front of the cephalothorax. Hobo spiders have two **chelicerae** with fangs attached to them. These fangs are used to **inject** the spider's **venom**.

Hobo spiders produce silk in glands located in their abdomen. Then they spin the silk from their **spinnerets**. These are fingerlike objects at the end of their abdomen.

The Body Parts of a Hobo Spider

Cephalothorax

Pedipalp

Abdomen

Chelicera

Leg

Spinneret

COLORS

Hobo spiders are dark-colored spiders. They are brown with gray markings. The underside of their abdomen often features a pattern of brown, gray, and tan.

The bottom of a hobo spider's **cephalothorax** has a stripe of light color down the middle. On the top, there is no set pattern. Their legs are all one color, unlike other funnel weaver spiders.

Hobo spiders do not have a set color or pattern. So, it is difficult to identify one by looking at it. Only an entomologist or arachnologist can determine the species by sight.

Opposite page: *An entomologist is a scientist who studies insects. A scientist who studies spiders and arachnids, such as this hobo spider, is called an arachnologist.*

WHERE THEY LIVE

Today, hobo spiders can be found in Europe and North America. In North America, they live as far south as Utah. They have moved as far north as the Canadian provinces of British Columbia and Alberta.

In Europe, these spiders live in fields, woods, and rock **quarries**. In North America, they live in wood piles, forest debris, and window wells. Sometimes hobo spiders move inside houses. Their favorite places are in basements and crawl spaces.

People often report finding hobo spiders in bathtubs or sinks. That is because the spider has fallen into these places. They cannot climb up through the drain. In fact, hobo spiders do not climb well at all.

Since they cannot climb, hobo spiders build webs on the ground. They prefer to build their webs in cool, moist areas. Their layered, flat webs have funnel-like lairs at the rear.

Female hobo spiders spend most of their lives in their webs. Male hobo spiders leave their webs when they become adults. Then, they go out in search of mates. This is usually when people find them.

Researchers believe hobo spiders are very adaptable. They can wander into many different environments and make a home.

SENSES

A hobo spider uses the hair on its body and legs to sense vibrations. It also uses the silk of its web to catch prey and avoid **predators**.

The silk of a hobo spider is a little different than the silk of most other spiders. A hobo spider's silk is not sticky. Instead, it has many strands. These strands trap an insect that is trying to walk through the web. When the insect struggles to free itself, the spider feels the vibrations.

Spiders have other sense organs besides their hair and webs. Hobo spiders have eight eyes grouped closely together in two rows. But they do not see objects well, even if they are just a few feet away.

Although hobo spiders cannot see, they can be frightened by light. Sometimes, hobo spiders freeze in place when a light turns on. The spider may become confused and run toward a person. The spider is actually scared. But, it seems like it is chasing the person.

Entomologists say hobo spiders are not afraid to attack. But, hobo spiders do not bite humans often. Usually, they only bite when they are trapped against someone's skin and cannot get away.

All funnel weaver spiders use their webs to sense vibrations.

DEFENSE

Spiders with sticky silk know how to avoid getting stuck in other spiders' webs. Hobo spiders do not. So, they often find themselves caught in sticky webs.

Praying mantises eat hobo spiders and other insects.

Predators of hobo spiders include wasps, praying mantises, birds, jumping spiders, and wolf spiders. Hobo spiders have encountered new predators as they moved closer to humans. House cats have been known to play with and kill hobo spiders.

Plus, many humans kill the spiders whenever they see them. People often do not realize how hobo spiders help reduce populations of insects and other spiders.

To avoid these threats, hobo spiders like to hide from anything that might hurt or eat them. The hobo spider's

Hobo spiders are nocturnal. That means they are active mainly at night. Wasps and mantises are active during the day. So, hobo spiders are somewhat safe from them.

coloring helps it hide. It likes to crawl underneath logs, rocks, and leaves.

Running is another defense of the hobo spider. They do not begin to run until they sense danger. Then they are very fast! A hobo spider can run as fast as 40 inches per second (102 cm/s).

FOOD

Hobo spiders have hearty appetites. They will eat just about anything they can catch and kill. They eat insects as well as other spiders.

A hobo spider sits in its lair and waits for prey. It rushes forward when an insect gets trapped in its web. The spider uses its fangs to stop and kill its victim. Then, the spider carries its prey back into the lair.

Once in the funnel-like pocket, the hobo spider **injects** its **digestive** juices into its victim. The juices dissolve the internal organs. The spider then sucks out the mush that remains.

Male hobo spiders have to be careful of females. Sometimes a male hobo spider wanders into a female's web. The male is just looking for a mate. Yet, he can become a meal for the female spider!

A hobo spider's bite is deadly to any animal without a backbone. A bite to a human will cause a large, oozing hole in the skin around the bite. The wound will heal in about 45 days.

BABIES

When a male hobo spider is ready to reproduce, he approaches a female's web. He then taps out a pattern of vibrations. If the female doesn't attack, the male enters the burrow.

Mating usually occurs in the fall. After mating, female hobo spiders lay their eggs in one to four egg sacs. These egg cases are made of layers of silk along with soil and debris. Each egg sac can hold 100 or more eggs.

Mother spiders attach their egg cases to the undersides of rocks or pieces of wood. It is rare for the spiders to lay their eggs inside houses. The eggs hatch in early summer.

The baby spiders, or spiderlings, spend their first year of life under rocks or other items. They molt, or lose their **exoskeleton**, several times during their first year. Then, the female spiderlings leave and build webs while males leave to find mates.

Funnel weaver spiders are a little different from most spiders. After mating, the adult male spider may stay with the female. The male hobo dies within months of mating. The female hobo spider dies soon after laying her eggs. So, the hobo spider's life span is about two years.

The female hobo spider may also attach her eggs to the crawl spaces of homes. But, rarely are hobo egg sacs found indoors.

GLOSSARY

arachnid (uh-RAK-nuhd) - an order of animals with two body parts and eight legs.

arthropod - a member of the phylum Arthropoda with an exterior skeleton.

bacteria - tiny, one-celled organisms that can only be seen through a microscope.

cephalothorax (seh-fuh-luh-THAWR-aks) - the front body part of an arachnid that has the head and thorax.

chelicera (kih-LIH-suh-ruh) - either of the leglike organs of a spider that has a fang attached to it.

digestive - of or relating to the breakdown of food into substances small enough for the body to absorb.

exoskeleton - the outer casing that protects an insect.

family - a group that scientists use to classify similar plants or animals. It ranks above a genus and below an order.

inject - to forcefully introduce a fluid into the body, usually with a needle or something sharp.

pedipalp (PEH-duh-palp) - either of the leglike organs of a spider that are used to sense motion and catch prey.

predator - an animal that kills and eats other animals.

quarry - a place where stone, slate, or limestone is dug, cut, or blasted out.

spinneret - either of the two body parts attached to the abdomen of a spider where the silk is made.

thorax - part of the front body of an arachnid that contains the head and lungs.

trait - a quality that distinguishes one person or group from another.

venom - a poison produced by some animals and insects. It usually enters a victim through a bite or sting.

WEB SITES

To learn more about hobo spiders, visit ABDO Publishing Company on the World Wide Web at **www.abdopub.com**. Web sites about these spiders are featured on our Book Links page. These links are routinely monitored and updated to provide the most current information available.

INDEX